Growth Mindset

7 Secrets to Destroy Your Fixed
Mindset and Tap into Your
Psychology of Success with Self
Discipline, Emotional Intelligence,
and Self Confidence

By Growth Mindset Academy,
Timothy Willink

Disclaimer

Table of Contents

Introduction

So often, we hear that we should dismiss our "fixed mindset" and open up to growth instead. Usually, many people pay little attention to this advice and chalk it up to the same breed of uselessly positive jargon, which will have no effect on our lives in the long run. However, the power of a growth mindset often means the difference between a person who can reach their goals and someone who always falls short. So, as much as we hear all these words, what do they actually mean? What's the real difference between growing always, and being tethered to the ground you walk on?

In most media we consume, we may see the stereotype of a genius character that doesn't let him be tethered by the ideas of what we should and shouldn't be how we should and shouldn't act. Some people demonize this kind of person and criminalize the act of rebelling against the standard set for us. Others, however, feel that there may be something to the theory that everything we do and know is wrong. It's these people, who reject our reality and substitute their own interpretation of it, who find it easier to adapt to a growth mindset.

However, you don't need to be a mad genius to fit a growth mindset into your daily life. Everyone and anyone can benefit from developing a growth mindset, and defeating your fixed mindset is a change which will benefit every kind of person, every personality, all walks of life, in everything they do. It's not easy to dig yourself out of the emotional pit of a fixed mindset, but it can be done with a little bit of determination.

Another stereotype we see in so much media, which is represented—although dramatized—by real people around us, is the classic example of the cynic. They have some kind of event in their past or with their life which has negatively affected them; they feel as though everything they do will land them back in the exact same spot in which they began. The cynic is also a fatalist, always believing that something that happens to them is always out of their control and that everything they ever do is destined to fail or be defeated by the will of someone else. Sometimes, people like this become annoyed by optimists who don't think the way that the cynic does.

While the cynic is so often disillusioned with the world that they've seemingly given up on putting forth any effort at all, the eccentric optimist formats the way the world works according to others, into their own perception and plans. Their plans for the world, to them, are the exact way in which they believe the actual events following will fall. Often times, there is absolutely nothing stopping an eccentric optimist from seizing the world and, in the worlds of Thoreau, "sucking the marrow out of life."

The cynic is the epitome and embodiment of a fixed mindset, while the eccentric optimist experiences the peak of what we would consider now a growth-oriented mindset. Understanding the applicable difference between these two kinds of people may also help you identify where you fall on that same spectrum of growth to fix.

This isn't to say that someone with a fixed mindset can truly never accomplish anything. While more extreme examples do experience that intense feeling of defeat, most don't. Most people today who experience a fixed mindset are simply following what they've been taught most of their life—if you don't succeed now, you would be better off giving up and trying something completely different.

Because of the way most education system functions, we seem to prioritize the efficiency of the future workforce above actually educating children and seeing them grow into that workforce. The student who is immediately successful is rewarded more than the student who fails over and over again before succeeding, even though the first child didn't actually learn anything in the process.

People who have a fixed mindset may not always feel stuck in one place, but they may feel as if they have no room for improvement, or have a hard time understanding the concept of personal growth. This is normal for many children, but those individuals who grow into adults with this sentiment can have trouble progressing through any part of their life. This includes work, higher education, or even their love life.

After all, why would you want to be with a partner who seems to have no ambition for bettering themselves and changing?

We don't understand ourselves very much these days. The world is so fast-paced and, for many, that's extremely overwhelming. The bustle of daily life is simply too much for many people to handle without help from others. Those other people are very different from you. Whether they have a growth mindset themselves or not, they're different from you and behave differently from you. Therefore, sometimes you have to meet in the middle for the people you love. Making that effort to compromise and change the way you think, if even just a little, for them, will mean the world to them and to you. That small shift may cause a chain of events which forever changes the way you perceive the world. That small shift may also end up coming around full circle, and helping the person you changed a little, to begin with. It's a very important part of our daily evolution.

Scientifically speaking, humans are done evolving for right now. According to any biology textbook you pick up, we haven't had any drastic evolutions in a while. However, the human race always changes a little. Every person on earth, whether they like it or not/know it or not, makes those same tiny little shifts throughout their lives to accommodate for choices they make and people they surround themselves with. It's hard to make all those changes so suddenly, so they take place over a massive stretch of time instead. Of course, even people with very fixed mindsets make those small changes often. They make these changes because they don't really recognize that they're happening. If a very close friend of yours has a certain funny habit, you may pick it up without noticing it. That small social adaptation is the kind of thing that we do throughout our entire lives in order to keep up with and understand the world. No matter how much you may think that nothing you do is permanent, many of those social adaptations follow you throughout your entire lifespan. Even though most of this change happens in our childhood or when we're otherwise fairly young, no one is resistant to change.

And the truth is we are still evolving every day in adulthood. No matter where in your life you are, or what you may be heading toward, you are always changing, and you hopefully always will be changing. This change is what allows you to learn more about yourself and the people you surround yourself with, and it allows you to increase your quality of life depending on how you adapt to those things. We change every day. If we don't change, the world changes with us, and we're always left in the dust. If you don't want to be left in the dust of the people you care about, read further and understand more about yourself and what it means to understand a growth mindset, and how to implement it into your personal world.

Thank you,

Xabier K. Fernao

Growth vs. Fixed Mindset

Now that we've gone over some of the classic examples of people who exhibit either an intensely fixed mindset or a very growth-oriented one, what's the actual difference between those two, and where may we see them in everyday life instead of in a novel?

Put simply, someone with a fixed mindset is someone who exhibits a lot of defeatist/fatalist attitudes, who feels as though nothing they do is permanent and that no matter how much they try, their built up skill will never be enough to match people with talent. People with a fixed mindset sometimes can have fairly low self-esteem and are maybe unconfident in their skills and abilities. They feel as though everything they do is destined to fail and be defeated by someone with a natural talent. The fixed mindset is not necessarily depressed but is someone who doesn't feel that their talents can change or develop.

Because we grow up in a world surrounded by people who get by only based off their talent, it isn't unreasonable to think that many people feel discouraged by these individuals who don't have to work for fame or attention from others. If you're someone who wants desperately to play a professional sport, and you're someone who practices relentlessly day in and day out, the last thing you need is to be shown up by someone who does the bare minimum and makes up for their lack of work in pure talent.

Seeing someone like that can be really infuriating, but don't be discouraged by what another person does to try and upstage you. Often, people who begin to fly on talent alone only sail smoothly for the beginning of their career. Later, if those same people don't also develop good work habits and good skills, they crash and burn.

Someone who exhibits more of a growth mindset is more confident in themselves and their abilities, finds they are more able to make clear and rational decisions that aren't clouded by their judgment, and is normally more guided by the hope of improvement than the anger they feel toward people who are given the natural advantage in life.

Someone with a growth mindset knows that they are more than capable of always growing and improving. They know how just hard it can be, but they know that the reward for the effort is the growth itself, and the satisfaction that comes with that growth.

Someone with a growth mindset isn't necessarily talented either. The difference between the growth mindset and the fixed one is not that the person with the growth mindset is talented—the difference is that the person with the growth mindset wants to work hard so that they can feel satisfied and know their own growth, instead of measuring their growth next to the growth of people who are already very talented. This person knows how to feel more secure in their own abilities—unlike the fixed mindset, who so often feels the need to prove themselves to those around them; for fear that they may find themselves falling behind their peers. This fear drives the fixed mindset to fight tooth and nail for everything. Although this is an improvement in its own way, its improvement in an unhealthy way, this kind of "improvement" does not inspire. It's not inspired in any way by a motivation to succeed and grow within the self. Instead, there's little growth at all. No matter how much physical growth goes on within that person, there's no real mental or psychological growth. Without that emotional development, physical development is effectively useless in the long run.

That's the real growth that matters, especially with regards to a fixed or growth mindset—it's all about how you grow in your head and in your heart. Although that sounds cliché, the most important part of growing as a person throughout your life is growing inside.

A fixed mindset may grow physically—it may grow a massive amount, physically—but they will never grow as much on the inside. A fixed mindset is just that, fixed, so it has a lower chance of ever changing or evolving, growing into a newer and better version of itself.

The growth mindset is the person who looks to improve themselves constantly, who is always able to be better and to help make improvements upon others. They're more apt to tricky situations because they were raised to be self-sufficient and capable. Those who are surer of themselves and more open to growth are also often the more successful individuals in their endeavors.

Part of whether a child naturally grows up with a fixed or growth mindset depends on the kind of parents that child had. If that child may have had parents who are more fatalistic themselves, they're more likely to have that same kind of attitude. Ideally, a child would have parents who foster all for their hopes and dreams and encourage them to chase their desires. With this kind of parenting, more children can adopt a more hopeful outlook.

A growth mindset makes a child who is able to socialize with others, someone who can be competitive and still lose fairly, and someone who can cooperate with many different kinds of people. A fixed mindset is someone who takes a much more negative approach to the competition, more often a sore loser, and usually tends to tether their self-worth to their status among their peers.

This makes them more likely to suffer from a material loss or a loss relating to status. It's much harder for people with fixed mindsets to bounce back from a loss, and much easier for them to spiral. They don't know how to lose, and they don't know how to recover from a loss. This means that people with fixed mindsets are more likely to spiral, which happens when a person suffers a loss and then accidentally begins to seek out another loss because they expect it. Being caught in this vicious cycle can result in a lot of negative outcomes, most of which end up with the person being in a depressed emotional state for extended periods of time.

That's really where developing the growth mindset starts--being able to admit that you have the capability to grow. Admitting to yourself and later understanding that you can't win at everything you do help you to be able to further foster your self-worth. Many people, especially young people, tether their confidence to things like a material victory, grades, or their social status. Connecting worth to things like this makes it exceedingly difficult for that person to disconnect, and then makes it harder for them to take a step back and have a more analytical look at themselves and their worth.

In a world where children are pushed more and more to grow up fast, they often don't have much time to learn where their worth should be tethered. Because of this quick adjustment, many kids make to the world; a lot of children grow into young adults with severe issues concerning their social skills.

These skills turn out to be crucial to their development, and the hindrance of them at an early age sets them that much further back in their emotional and social development. This phase of their lives can become the one kids get stuck in for some time, making them more open to the belief that they will never progress forward. This repeated failure, or the belief of it, can quickly spiral and turn into a fixed mindset.

Not only that, but it can become a fixed mindset that prevents the person from socially developing for a while. Young children don't often show whether or not they will grow into people with fixed or growth mindsets, but most children display personality traits that are more commonly found in fixed mindsets because they are still in their very early staged of developing socially. They steal from others and become easily upset when they don't succeed.

This frustration is found in everyone, but the ability to deal with and rationalize that frustration is what separates a healthier child from a less healthy one. In the sense of emotional and social capability, the growth mindset is the kind of child who is willing to share and who can deal with rejection from peers. A child who has trouble with that kind of thinking is more prone to being melodramatic and feeling that, because they were rejected by their peers, they now have inherently less worth because of this interaction. Tethering the self-worth and confidence to social status is a massive downfall of individuals with fixed mindsets, if only because they suffer so much for it with no benefit to match it. That suffering drives the fixed mindset to fall apart at the seams, spiraling more and more into the feeling of constantly being defeated and worthless.

That feeling of worthlessness, rock bottom, is the place which defines the exact difference between someone who can develop a growth mindset at that moment, and someone who is still deeply entrenched in their fixed mindset. That place where everyone is in deep despair—where everything has gone totally wrong. That's the place where every motivational book and video tells you to dig deep, find out what you're made of, and so on and so forth. While hearing that mantra over and over again gets annoying, it's true that you are defined by your darkest moments.

A trauma victim is not defined by their trauma—they are defined by how they respond to that trauma moving forward. Someone who simply gives up and allows that trauma, that dark place, to overwhelm their lives, is someone who may not believe that they can even get better. A victim who copes with their trauma and who acknowledges it without letting it consume them is someone who knows how to grow and move on and respond accordingly to terrible things.

As often as we hear father figures say it over and over, life really isn't fair—not at all, in the slightest, not one bit of it is fair. You can try to make it fair, but it won't work. The thing about that is that when you see something in your life that very obviously isn't fair, you have little choice other than to press on and keep going, despite that unfairness.

Think about a time when the odds were stacked against you. Whether in a genuine competition or a point in your career or personal life where you felt the entire thing was rigged against you, where you felt you were destined to fail. Did you keep going despite all that adversity? If you did, you're someone who knows how to deal with adversity and overcome it. That specific point in time didn't necessarily define you as a person, but it shows you that you are willing to try and overcome unfairness and adversity. This is one of the many traits that are so admirable about people with growth mindsets.

It's so very easy to give up. It's not difficult to stop resisting adversity, and it isn't difficult to stop trying. It is difficult, however, to force through even though you know it isn't a good idea. It's hard to push through the diversity in your way, but someone has to do it. Sometimes, "someone," must be you.

The goal, if you currently have a more fixed mindset, is to progress on the spectrum from that fixed mindset to a growth mindset. That can be hard, but most certainly not impossible. Reading this, to begin with, shows that, at the very least, you have something of an interest in a growth mindset and how you can develop one. The first step of adopting a growth mindset is shaking off the effects that a fixed mindset can have on you.

It's important, firstly, to make the distinction that having a fixed mindset does not make you lesser, or sadder, or in any way inferior to someone with a growth mindset. A fixed mindset is a mindset in which someone believes that their skills and talents are stagnant and permanent. Having a fixed mindset means some of these things for you;

- Having a fixed mindset is not something evil, but it is something to avoid—people with fixed mindsets are in no way bad people, but the ideal for any person is that they have a growth mindset so they can change and evolve as people much easier. It's a good idea to avoid a "fixed mindset" thought the way that you would avoid other negative thoughts that plague your life. However, don't demonize someone who is stuck in a fixed mindset themselves. It's harder for some to break out of that cycle of defeatist thinking that it is for their peers.

- Someone with a fixed mindset is not usually someone who is sad or bitter—although sometimes, people with severely fixed mindsets can come off as bitter or depressed, that has no correlation with the actual definition and application of "fixed mindset". Those with fixed mindsets believe that their skills can't improve, not that they can never be good at anything. Try to keep this in mind when addressing someone with a fixed mindset—they aren't a lost cause or someone suffering from an illness, so don't treat them as if they're someone with a condition.

- From the perspective of someone with a fixed mindset who wants to foster a growth mindset, consider times in your life when you've undergone change—there are definitely many examples you could draw from, as everyone in their life goes through many different phases and changes, both physically and emotionally. These changes help you to adapt, but they also allow you to improve your existing skills. So, that in and of itself may disprove your theory that all your personality traits and intelligence are stagnant.

- Your brain undergoes a lot of shifts too—in more recent scientific years, we've discovered the extent to which the human mind can retain and change to suit the needs of an individual. Also referred to as "brain plasticity," the ability for your brain to change drastically is also indicative that you are also subject to dramatic and great change.

- You become smarter even after your brain stops developing—even though most brains stop aging around the age of 25, all brains keep going after that, as long as the brain is normal and without complication. Assuming this is the case, you still retain more and more information as you learn and grow older. So, even though your brain can change drastically in your younger years, you don't stay the exact same in terms of intelligence afterward. Where did you think the stereotype of older people and all their wisdom came from?

- You are just as smart as the person sitting next to you, and that's subject to change—scientifically speaking, your intelligence is very fluid and kind of unreliable way of measuring how well you do in certain areas of life which you may not ever actually encounter. You are likely just as applicable smart as anyone in the room with you, or anyone in your friend group. You may, in some ways, be both the smartest and the least intelligent person in your whole town or city. All of that is subject to change, so don't worry about it too much. Everything you do or don't do may have an impact on your intelligence, and it may now. Realistically, there's no true way to fairly and accurately measure the raw intellect of every human on Earth, for many reasons. So, the belief that your intelligence can never change is not only fatalistic, but it's also scientifically void.

- There are many different kinds of intelligence—whether you be socially or emotionally intelligent, "book" smart, or very skilled at working with your hands, you are very intelligent in some way or another. This is one of the reasons that most intelligence tests don't actually measure your true capabilities. Instead, they measure what they conceivably can and call it a day. While this is efficient, it does little to actually tell you about yourself and your room for improvement.

- Speaking of which, there is always room for improvement—you can't win them all. You can try and try in anything you please for as long as you want, but there's a very small chance that you will win your very first time, and there's also a very small chance that your winning streak will be very long in anything you do. That's purely up to simple probability, as has little to do with your intelligence or skill. You simply can't be perfect the first time you commit to a task, and you can't be perfect every time you do something. The world is in no way rigged against you if it doesn't permit you the win that you want, whenever you want it. It's childish to think that you will always be the best, so try improving your skills on your off time instead. Even if that improvement doesn't yield many results in the way of winning medals, it will yield results for your own personal satisfaction.

- Your achievements should matter to you always, no matter whether or not you "won" - -even if it's not something you can win or lose, your idea of how successful you are should never be tethered in something like social status or your place on a podium. It's the skills that you create and harness for yourself that serve you in the long-term, not the medal and the plaque you may win and be proud of at the moment. Of course, be proud of your accomplishments. Often, our accomplishments let us know that our hard work is paying off, but make sure that you don't let those accomplishments define how you feel about yourself and your skills.

- Take pride in whatever you want— sometimes, whether we have a growth mindset or a fixed one, we sometimes get hung up on what we can and can't take pride in. Some accomplishments may feel as though they're things we'll be laughed at or ridiculed for. However, anything you feel proud of yourself for achieving is more than enough to be proud of over. One of the main functions of society is to push down things that it deems unfit for praise. It's the prideful rebellion of people who enjoy things that are looked down upon that changes the course of that society.

- There are a lot of misconceptions about changing your mindset and attitude—many people dismiss the actual weight and merit of your perception of the world and how you relate to the world. This may because we've been treating the concept of "attitude" as laughable since middle school. However, as we grow older, it becomes more and more obvious that everything we do has an indirect or direct impact on the way we treat ourselves and others. So, educating everyone you can about what growth and fixed mindsets actually mean can have a large impact on how we think about these mindsets in regard to our mental health as a society.

- It's more than ok to have a bad day every now and then—even people who are the most motivated have terrible days throughout the course of their lives. It's something that comes naturally to most all people in the world, no matter how much of a growth mindset they may have. Try not to let it disrupt your pattern of improvement. A bump in the road doesn't derail you.

- Improvement is in no way linear or constant—there is no one on Earth who has tried to get better at something or heal from something, who has gotten better every day. With any kind of condition, any scenario, any occurrence, people have days where they may even get worse than when they started. Working your way through a difficult time is daunting, and not something easily did alone. Trusting in people, trusting in yourself, and trusting that you know what you're doing, will all be what helps you through the most difficult parts of breaking out of your unhealthy habits.

With all of this in mind, move forward knowing that a fixed mindset is not a pest or a virus to get rid of. Like many things, it's something that needs to take time to evolve into something bigger and better than its original form. Sure, it can be very difficult to see the end result when it isn't right in front of you.

Many challenges you face will be like a marathon— long and grueling, and without any foreseeable end for a little while. However, the longer you forge onward, the closer you get to see the end. Once you see the end, the closer you get to be at that end. Even at the "end," you need to keep growing and improving even past that finish line. To stop and give up after finishing would defeat the purpose of even beginning the journey in the first place. So, to reach the finish line comfortably, forge on at a steady pace and try not to burn yourself out. If you work hard and pace yourself, reaching that daunting finish line may turn out to be a lot easier than you thought.

Being able to grow and develop as a person, both you and for others is one of the many rewards of developing a growth mindset. Being able to adapt to different situations which you encounter in your life as an adult—and being able to start harnessing the skills to do so earlier on in your life—helps you build bonds faster and be more versatile in all areas of life, from your personal relationships to the workforce.

There are a lot of nuances that go into breaking out of the dangerous habits that so often befall people who have very fixed mindsets. There's a lot of misunderstanding of what it actually means to have a fixed or a growth mindset, and it can be very difficult to dispel all of those rumors and that entire stigma. Nevertheless, taking the time to actually understand everything you can about how to change your mindset and attitude for the better will undoubtedly help you to become a better and much better-rounded person. It will also, of course, help you to be more open to all kinds of growth.

The 7 Rules of Growth

There are many things that go into changing yourself and your attitude for the better. As you've read, it's a slow and arduous journey for everyone who embarks on it, and sometimes it can seem as though the journey isn't worth the reward, to begin with. Of course, once that destination of a growth mindset comes into view, the fruits of the labor somehow become magically much sweeter very quickly.

There are seven main rules to follow while you embark on the journey to a growth mindset. These are the following:

1. Ask yourself questions, don't relay statements. Something a lot of people with fixed mindsets do, is they say things to themselves and insist on things to others that may simply not be very true at all. In fact, most statements made about their abilities by people with fixed mindsets happen to be wrong more often than right. For instance, instead of saying "I'm not good at math"-- a statement that has no basis or meaning other than the insistence of the person saying it—try asking yourself what you can do to improve at math, or what you're doing wrong. There's so much you can do then, to solve your own problems. The issue arises when someone complains about

the issues they face, and yet does nothing to try and better themselves or work on solving the problem that is in front of them, and which is usually very solvable. If you feel that you have an underlying issue, don't chalk up all your misfortune related to it by casting aside all your issues. Instead, ask yourself what you can do about it instead of passively watching your problems grow larger and more daunting by the moment. With each of those passing moments, there is also a moment that passes you by in which you can stand up and take an active role in your own life. While yes, that's very hard to do for most people, it's not impossible. It only becomes hard when you're actually forced to commit to it. Simply standing up and telling yourself that something is going to be done is the very important first step, and it's very easy in and of itself. It's the work you have to do immediately afterward that requires more precision and grueling work. Asking yourself questions you can solve, presenting yourself with fluid problems with fluid solutions helps you to move through all those problems much faster. Additionally, tack on "yet" to your statements, if you feel the need to make them. "I'm not good at math yet." is a statement, not a question, but it's a statement that clearly alludes to the fact that you will be improving very soon. Although it isn't much, that single word can mean the difference between feeling defeated and feeling invigorated. Not being able to do something is discouraging, but not being able to do something "yet" can be uplifting in its own right.

2. While it's important to stay fluid, an important distinction to make between growth and fixed mindsets is that a growth mindset is informed only by data and never be any other kind of information. Keep in mind that it's still very important to keep options open and be open to information from all sources. Ultimately, however, it's exceedingly important that your opinion be well-informed and based in fact alone. If you allow your information to be even partially made up of the opinion of someone else, you are likely going to be at least partially incorrect in your assumption of that situation. No matter who is involved in a certain party or situation never trusts the word of someone else unless you can fact-check it in whatever way is easiest. Even if you hear simple news from a friend that may be important to you, look up the actual information online to be sure that you and your friend aren't being misinformed. This is in no way assuming that any of your peers may be actually trying to trick you or

manipulate you. This is simply assuming that many people in the world are mildly misinformed every day of their lives, including you and me. So, make sure you do everything you can to combat that potential for misinformation. People with growth mindsets are typically more likely to be skeptical of the information they receive through word of mouth, so they're much more likely to back of up thoughts with factual information instead of opinion. Of course, this makes the fixed mindset seem marginally more trusting, but not to the extent which would require the fixed mindset to completely accept everything that is told for them. This is also not assuming that fixed mindsets are gullible enough to believe anything that's ever said to them. It's only to warn against otherwise naive and sometimes gullible people. Someone with a strong growth mindset is more than willing to fact check everything said to them by essentially everyone.

3. Small things lead to bigger things which lead to big things—it's easy to chalk up most things to being worthless if, on the surface, those things appear to be very small. However, compounding small things with consistency soon turns those many small things into a big thing which is no longer insignificant, and which now has a lasting

impression on your life. This is the basic method of compounding, a method which is utilized in most fields modernly. Essentially, the method begins with a small task for every day, which the user implements consistently. After that small task is easily managed, more small tasks are piled on as well. This step is repeated until most, if not all, of the workload, is on the shoulders of the recipient, but they feel less stress because of that slow but steady compounding. Adding slight pressure over time will not break wood but smashing it quickly will. So, this method of slow but steady progress works on all kinds of people with all kinds of jobs, including ones that pertain to changing the lifestyle in any way. This would, of course, expand to changing from a fixed mindset to a growth one. You could begin with a very small assignment for every day, such as teaching yourself to ask questions instead of providing statements pertaining to your skills. Over time, consistently keeping up with that habit will feel easier and easier over time. So, once that habit comes as second nature to you, add on another habit which will hopefully work toward breaking some of the other habits you may have as someone with a fixed mindset. After a while, ideally, you'll be in a mental space where you're able to manage many tasks at once while keeping up with normal responsibilities. This is a more efficient and constant way of keeping yourself in check while staying firmly on track toward your destination of a growth mindset. It doesn't necessarily matter what each tier of your daily responsibilities is, so you can make it up as you go according to what you think you can comfortably handle. If you want more of a challenge, you can force yourself to carry more responsibilities more often. If you have a busier workday, you can settle for a limited number of responsibilities which you switch out for every few days. It can be had to keep up with everything that goes on around you, and it can also be very tough to keep up with your own standards for yourself. Remember that you are the one in control for your journey and your goals, so you're also the one responsible if you fall off track. This method is for people who are absolutely committed to a growth mindset and who are able to be very responsible and consistent for extended periods of time.

4. Never, ever, settle for sub-par work. This can be interpreted as less directed toward people with a fixed mindset and simply people who are lazier workers, but the phrase "this will do" has to become your worst enemy when you want to adopt a growth mindset. Hating

the idea of settling for average, settling for less, is part of what sets growth mindsets apart from the rest of the pack. While someone with a fixed mindset is more likely to settle for something they know will probably get a fine grade, but isn't their best work, a growth mindset will be more inclined to go above and beyond the call of duty to fulfill and exceed the expectation they have for themselves, because that's exactly what it means to always be growing. To always be growing and evolving and getting better means that you have to have high standards for any of your work, no matter what kind of work it is. A growth mindset is willing to put their everything into even a relatively simple project because they want to see if they can exceed their own expectations. An ideal growth mindset is genuinely curious to see what they can do if they invest all their energy into performing well. Of course, a lot of students and employees find it hard to suddenly switch over to this kind of energy if they've been going their entire career drifting by on something, they know is okay. They're consciously aware that they could do better, but they likely don't care enough about the final grade to put forth any more effort. So, don't make the satisfaction about the grade or the expectation of the superior authority.

Instead, make the reward for an outstanding job something physical, if you need to, like a snack or a break from work quickly. After finishing a few math problems, taking a moment to get up, walk around the room, and stretch can really be so incredibly good for anyone, no matter how long they've been at the desk or what kind of work they may have been doing. Or, if you want, you can make satisfaction something much more personal. Make the satisfaction of a job well done resonate not necessarily with the teacher or the boss, but with you. There's no one who can better predict the way you perform and feel better than yourself, neither cater to your own emotional needs before the emotional requirements of the people around you.

5. Really and genuinely get every single lesson you can from everything that ever happens to you--the point of living, to some, is to grow constantly and learn from everything. Adopt this kind of enthusiasm and be able to adopt every piece of advice you can possibly draw from a situation. Whether it be something more superficial, like a small misfortune, or a real and genuinely heartbreaking loss, there's something to be learned from absolutely every situation, every scenario. Look through the sequence of events and pick out what happened to you and why it may have

meaning. Look for a way you can learn a valuable lesson in a situation where you feel very plainly wrong. It may be hard at first, but I promise there's something very valuable to be learned in all of these tiny defeats. Eventually, after you internalize enough of these lessons and actually put them to use, you can grow immensely as a person—you may find that after a while you see a whole new person when you look in the mirror. Sure, it's really difficult for a defeatist to look into the mirror as say to themselves, "It doesn't matter what actually happened to me if I can't learn from it." This especially comes into play with a fixed mindset that loves to fixate on their own misfortune. This is not necessarily what a fixed mindset is, but the kind of person who fixates on their own grief and very rarely fixates on the issues of others is someone who most definitely has a fixed mindset. They're someone who's usually pretty unwilling to put in the effort to improve their situation because so much of their emotional revenue comes from all of their plights. Nevertheless, if you're someone who wants to be able to develop their growth mindset, actively seek out lessons in the world around you. After a little bit of practice, they become much easier to find and you may even have learned something very sentimental to boot. Don't knock the pursuit of knowledge, no matter where that pursuit actually takes place and what that pursuit is the pursuit of.

6. Humiliation and embarrassment are a large part of your life. It feels terrible to be humiliated by people you likely look up to, but throughout the most of your life, it's going to happen to you more than once, yes, it's something that everyone really wants to avoid, but it's unavoidable for most. So, don't feel as though you have to work every day to avoid being embarrassed or humiliated. Our current society works hard to shame people for not immediately knowing things at the exact same time as everyone else. This can really pressure that outsider, make them feel incredibly unintelligent, and force them to further isolate themselves from the pack. Additionally, there are many people who, despite people's best recommendations, may give up once they feel ridiculed. This kind of person with a fixed mindset is very likely to be found outside the back feeling sorry for themselves because they want to wait for somebody to comfort them. The truth is you're very rarely going to have your own personal comforter for everything you do wrong and everything you say out of place. Often, you have to bite the bullet and apologize for your own mistakes. Or, if you

didn't necessarily make a mistake, but you were humiliated, you sometimes have to just keep going about your business as though everything you do is as it should naturally be. When we're embarrassed, we often get the impression that people are watching us or actively mocking us, but this isn't usually the case. Usually, it's just a matter of people being interested in what you're doing and how you're reacting. Although, usually people aren't really looking at you at all. If the embarrassment was truly over something that mattered so much, somebody would say something to you, and you may be asked to say something publicly to apologize. This is rarely the case, however, so most cases just end in feeling paranoid and as though everyone has their eye on you. We think that our public embarrassment was the highlight of that person's day, so of course, they're watching us. However, this is rarely the case, and so the best way to deal with that familiar red flush of hot shame is to simply keep going about your day as though nothing had even happened. Eventually, anything that transpired becomes lost to time, quickly forgotten by most people in attendance. This ability, to cope with loss and with embarrassment, can make you falter at times; it's hard to handle that humiliation for a lot of people. However, someone with a strong growth mindset is able to push through that humiliation because of the respect they have for themselves and others, and because of their humility.

7. Finally, be open to new things, people, and experiences that may jump into your life. Some people aren't naturally extraverted, so they have trouble joining social spaces and entertaining people at the levels that some of them are more socially outgoing peers. So, when a very introverted person, or even just someone who finds themselves socially awkward, come across a person who is more than willing to befriend them and care for them, they may actually have a lot of trouble making friends with that person. Even though this very valuable thing is presented in front of you, it can be extremely difficult for someone who suffers from social anxiety, or even just a severe introvert with little social experiment, to take the plunge and try to befriend them and bond with that person. They're likely someone who's tried making friends before and who may have been very harshly rejected in the past. Of course, no one wants to go through that more than they have to, so they may shut off their social impulses to everyone around them. This way, they don't have to even think about the potential

of being rejected by this new person, because they aren't even their friend. If anything, it's now them who are rejecting the new person walking into their life. The same principle can be easily applied to things like work ideas and advice. We usually don't really want to follow up on ideas unless they come from us, because we like to think that we're original and intelligent and creative enough to come up with everything on our own, all the time. This simply can't be the case every single time someone needs a new idea or advice. As much as we may want to be the most helpful, most intelligent person in the whole world, thinking we can achieve this is more than a little gullible of us. Sure, it's a nice feeling to be recognized for helping others, but it's also nice for those others to be recognized for similar actions. There's more than enough mutual knowledge, experience, and ideas in the world for more than one person to share it. Keep in mind that everyone around you has different experiences and different minds, so they're more prone to different ideas than you. You haven't experienced the entirety of history unfold, and you haven't experienced everything that's ever happened to anyone, so it's probably significantly harder for you to come up with the kind of ideas that other people are having. At the same time, though, all other people likely have a harder time coming up with ideas like yours as well. So many people spend so much of their time chasing other people's dreams and ideas, that it's hard for us to stop and appreciate our own mind and our own ideas. So, whenever you feel hopeless and jealous of the ideas of someone near you, take a moment and meditate on that feeling. Breathe deeply and reflect on yourself and why you feel the way you do. It's likely that all those jealous feelings are hurting you from the inside, and you may not have even realized it. In fact, many people who feel this way tend to drown out their feelings with how they feel, ironically. They mask the sadness they feel when they feel like they've been outdone with the bitter anger, or just the feeling of jealousy, that comes with those feelings. Surely, those feelings you have aren't necessarily conducive to your growth mindset or to your positive outlook on life. Therefore, try whenever you can to meditate on the things you feel. When you're able to identify exactly what you think you feel, you're also more able to figure out what you want to do about those feelings. Those feelings can be tricky and difficult to get rid of, but don't falter. As hard as it can be to get rid of these pervasive feelings of jealousy, remind yourself when you meditate on negative feelings that you are equal to all your peers, in mind and in spirit. Everything you create can be just as beautiful and creative as something that comes from the person next to you. It can be hard to believe that if you're someone who is still learning how to untie their self-worth from their materialistic achievements, but working at it a little bit each day is the best way for you to improve quickly. That improvement may be the exact thing that unlocks the door to your growth mindset. Stay focused.

On top of all these rules, something very important that should be addressed but may not necessarily need to be added as a rule—take care of yourself and love yourself in any way you know how. There are so many ways in which you are someone very worthy of love and support, and there are so many ways in which you should practice self-love and self-care. Those with very severely fixed mindsets and even those who are hyper-fixated on growth may find themselves neglecting themselves and their responsibilities to themselves and their bodies.

You are much more important than your grades, your achievements, and your social status. The fact that you are a living and breathing person grants you so much free will and so much capability, that to squander it would be a shameful waste of ability.

Even if the way you care for yourself seems small and insignificant, it's a way for you to monitor your health and practice something very important to you—being kind to everyone includes being kind to yourself.

Sometimes, people with very fixed mindsets can be very tough on themselves because they hold themselves to the same "standard" that they perceive everyone else to reside at. It's usually very hard to reach this pretend standard, and it's sometimes impossible for you to come close to the standard.

Try your hardest to disregard the standard, and instead take a look at yourself, and say something kind. Even if your goal for a day is to not be harsh and cruel to yourself, that's enough to start out with. Working your way up, compounding, being kind to yourself is the way to truly lift yourself out of the emotional shackles that a defeatist attitude may place you into.

Everything about you is fluid because you're someone very free in a very free world. Take advantage of the space you live in and try to take little moments every single day to be kinder to yourself.

These are rules to follow, but you don't have to follow all of them right away. That seems like a very laborious task all at once, so it's alright if you just skip to working at growing your skills and abilities. The people you surround yourself with, and the rules they follow, will also have an impact on you and your personal rules. So, try not to be too harsh on yourself or on others. Being kind is the key to growing, much like a plant. If you refuse to water it or feed it, how can you ever expect it to grow?

Conclusion

The path to growth can be daunting for many, and some people truly don't seem themselves as cut out for it, at least not in this part of their life. Truly, there's no way to be completely closed off the change. It happens all around us, constantly, all the time. Change happens around us and inside us. Growth, too, happens all around us and within us, both in the physical and the spiritual.

It's never a bad idea to try and make the most of this growth, really. It's unavoidable, and the world is much less rigid than it may appear, so what of it, really? We're all just learning how to be human on Earth, and that feeling brings much camaraderie. In a way, the growth of the individual also inspires the growth of the group. Growth of the group also inspires the growth of the individual, so many people say we simply go around and around in a never-ending cycle. If we do, why are so many people hung up on change?

Truth be told, people are deathly afraid of change. It's just something that happens so often in life and is so unexpected, many people are afraid of change—you are probably afraid of change to a degree. It's a simple fear and one that most need help to overcome. Many people need to be reassured that change in their life is more positive than negative and thinking that way brings a lot of people more joy in their lives.

Their growth brings them joy--their development as people bring them more joy than the despair brought to them by the loss they may suffer from change. In a way, people who believe they can never change may simply believe that because they're afraid of change. Most, however, are simply of the belief that the world is a purely analytical place full of numbers and code— that the emotion and empathy only serve as a distraction from those things.

This simply isn't true, of course. It's hard to accept that things are much less black and white than we may originally think, but its fact that everything you experience is a mixture of those emotions and those numbers together. Many people don't want to think about the numbers and the mathematics part of life. Many people don't want to consider the emotional, sentimental, and empathetic part of life. These two concepts create a juxtaposition which adds color to our world, which inspires change and growth within the Earth's inhabitants.

And how do we, its inhabitants, respond to that call? Hopefully, many of us respond positively, growing and flourishing, coming into our own as we age. Unfortunately, some of us do not exactly flourish at all on Earth. Many of us feel easily wronged and lament about how unfair the Earth truly is. Many try to uncover the dark secret behind society, to no avail. Because the secret is already out. We're both constantly open to change, and constantly afraid of what that change brings us.

So, I raise you this parting question: what are you chasing after? What is it that keeps you awake at night, tossing and turning, nervous to get at it? What is that ambition, where is it, what is it going toward?

Thinking about your ambition every day can hopefully serve as a good reminder to you and to others that nothing you do should be done without reason, nothing you do should be done without passion or ambition of some kind. If you live any part of your life, really, without any sort of passion, you become a passive observer to everything that goes on in your life.

Every relationship, every opportunity, passes you by without that passion. Some people find it insanely difficult to conjure up any sort of passion for anything, really. Some people find it simple, muscle memory, second nature to live and breathe in the heat of the moment for their entire lives.

For people who don't exist for their passion, try to find it as best you can. Once you do find it, try your hardest to latch onto it as hard as you can, for as long as you can. The longer you have a tight grip on your passion, the more you can direct toward wherever you want it to lead you. You play an active role in your own life, so please don't ever be afraid to grab the bull by the horns and forge your own path.

Additional questions, for those who have found their passion or passions already—do you have a passion for growth? If not, why not? Isn't growth what we're inspired by with every day? Isn't growth the very thing that allows us to make friends and new connections every day of our lives? It's so difficult for us to make connections and improvements to ourselves without a certain passion for growth. So, if you don't have some kind of passion for growth, you'd do well to try and find it, and take advantage of it as soon as you can.

After all, growth is our drive. Growth is our life. We're always changing and evolving, inside and out, trying desperately and fighting to keep up with the entire world. That can be incredibly stressful, so many of us may turn ourselves away from growth in an attempt to resign ourselves to simply letting things happen to us as doing nothing about it.

If you think this method of dealing with your strife is going to get you anywhere, you're sorely mistaken. Resigning yourself to passive submission is the wrong way to take a break from your busy life. Instead, care for yourself and get back up and keep going as soon as you feel ready. After all, you've got a whole world out there to grow with.

FREE BONUS

P.S. Is it okay if we overdeliver?

I believe in overdelivering way beyond our reader's expectations. Is it okay if I overdeliver?

Here's the deal, I am going to give you an extremely valuable cheatsheet of "Accelerated Learning"...

What's the catch? I need to trust you... You see, my team and I wants to overdeliver and in order for us to do that, we've to trust our reader to keep this bonus a secret to themselves. Why? Because we don't want people to be getting our ultimate accelerated learning cheatsheet without even buying our books itself. Unethical, right?

Ok. Are you ready?

Simply Visit this link:
http://bit.ly/acceleratedcheatsheet

Everything else will be self explanatory after you've visited: http://bit.ly/acceleratedcheatsheet

We hope you'll enjoy our free bonuses as much as we've enjoyed preparing it for you!

Free Preview of the Book "Alpha Male Confidence" by Timothy Willink

Chapter 1: What is an Alpha Male?

We live in a time and age where we are just regular people, walking around the street, not knowing what to do with our life. The thing is, many people don't know what they want to do with their life because they have no guidance and don't know how to get somewhere based on society's stigmas. There are millions of people living like this, and out of those millions, there is one who is an alpha male. An alpha male is someone who's on top of the game and knows what he's doing with his life. He also knows what to do when it comes to changing for the better and to make his dreams come true. For many people that don't know where the term alpha came from, it simply means g the top of the food chain or the top person in the tribe. The term alpha male has been used in animals for a long time now, many of the chimpanzees are the lions who are the king of the pride are known as the alpha male. An alpha male is someone who is the king of the pride and takes care of everyone in the pride, protecting anyone from any danger. In the animal world, the strongest animal is known as the alpha male.

The animal who is the strongest and can fight off any other dangers that they might occur, on the other hand, a male has to be an alpha. Many of the people are saying that females are "alpha female." They can be in certain tribes; however, in the animal kingdom, the alpha is always a male. In the animal kingdom when an animal is turned into an alpha male, they get the preference in the foods that they're going to be eating and also get the preference and terms off the female they're going to be getting. Being an alpha male in the animal world gives you every right to make with any female your mate. Essentially, an alpha male gets whatever he wants whenever he wants. If you want to be an alpha male, then you need to be a powerful person both mentally and physically, to become an alpha male.

However, this does not mean that you're going to be an alpha male. Being an alpha male requires a lot of things to be in order when it comes to getting the top of the food chain. If size mattered, an elephant would have been the king of the jungle, but instead, it is the lion. Physical dominance does matter when it comes to becoming an alpha male. However, there's a lot of aspects to consider before you think that you're going to be an alpha male. An alpha male is someone who's winning the race in life. Meaning that he's doing whatever he can to make his life the "dream life," he wants it to be, someone fearless when it comes to achieving whatever goal it is that he is trying to achieve. This chapter will give you a great idea of where you are in your life, and how you can change it to become a better alpha male.

Everybody has what it takes to become an alpha male. However, you need to understand some basic rules when it comes to becoming one as it is imperative that you understand the characteristics behind an alpha male. Later on in this book, we're going to give you a lot of ideas on how to become an alpha male. However, just understand the basics and then go from there. With that being said, let's get into the topic of who was in an alpha male and what characteristics they show. One of the greatest things when it comes to becoming an alpha male is the fact that they're happy with their life.

If you are an alpha male, then most likely you are happy with your life, and where you're going, More specifically you don't feel tired on the weekdays, and you don't get excited for the weekends. Many people who get excited about the weekends are not happy with their life, their weekend is their escape from real life. If you feel like that, then there's a high chance that you are not going in the right direction in regards to achieving your goal on living the best life, which makes it impossible for you to become an alpha male. One of the biggest thing when it comes to being an alpha male is knowing what you're doing and going in the right direction, so being happy and going the right direction with your life is very important when it comes to becoming an alpha male.

Another thing that makes you an alpha male is the fact that you are in control with your life. I'm sure you've heard your friend say this before. They might be telling you that they are not in control of their life, and they don't know what they're going to be doing with their life. This is the case for most people, unless you're an alpha male, then you know what you're doing with your life, and you're happy with it. As we told you previously, you need to be happy with your life, and for you to be happy with your life, you need to know what you're doing with your life. You need to make sure you have your life figured out when it comes to what you want in your life and when it comes to career. Many people think that it is tough to understand what you want to do with your life. In fact, it is one of the simplest things to understand, sit down, and ask yourself what your dream job was when you were younger.

By younger I mean when you were in your teenage years, whatever the answer is chances are you still want to do that however you have buried on your dreams to become that because you think it is impossible to become a certain person. If you think like that, then there's a high chance that you are not an alpha male. Which is why you need to change this as soon as possible and start pursuing your lifelong dream of becoming whatever it is that you want to be. If you want to be an actor, then go ahead to become an actor, make sure that you pursue it fully and never give up. With that being said another thing when it comes to becoming an alpha male, is that you get things done. As we told you previously that you need to be following your lifelong dream when it comes to becoming whatever it is that you want to be.

You are not going to get there by sitting on your butt, you need to make sure that you're taking actions of making it happen, finding out how to get there as one of the most crucial things when it comes to becoming an alpha male. It is not that you get there, it is a fact that you try and get there. Trying is one of the most important things when it comes to becoming an alpha male, many people who don't try feel like they haven't done anything in their life, and they feel terrible about themselves. Which is not the case when it comes to becoming an alpha male, an alpha male will do whatever it takes to pursue their dreams, whether it is impossible by many people.

The Impossible word does not exist when you're an alpha male, you make it happen whatever it is that you're trying to do. If you say, you're going to do something you get it done, plain and simple.

Another thing that alpha male takes care of is the people around him. One of the things of being an alpha male is to take care of your pride. In later chapters were going to show you how to understand your pride and who it is that you need to take care of, as there are many imposters that you need to get rid of as soon as possible. However, once you find out the people you need to take care of you will within a heartbeat. Truth be told, if you want to be an alpha male, then you need to take care of your family and your friends the right way. since you will be the leader of your pact, you need to share your success with your friends and family and make it happen for them and for you.

Also, you need to help all the people in your pride to become successful just like you. This is one of the most important traits when it comes to becoming an alpha male when you're an alpha male not only you're helping yourself become better, but you're also helping others who are in your circle. An alpha male will never hate on someone else's success or bring anybody else down.

In fact, an alpha male will bring everybody up and help them become more successful in whatever it is that they're doing. One thing that makes an alpha male is the ability to help others make sure they consider that and understand that when it comes to becoming an alpha male. When it comes to becoming an alpha male, you also need to be playing high-risk high-reward games.

Meaning that you cannot accept to become an alpha male if you don't have to tenacity to become whatever it is that you want to be, simply put you will not work for anybody else. An alpha male is his own boss, which means that he will take no crap from anybody. If you want to be an alpha male, that means that you will have to risk everything to get everything if that makes sense to you. You cannot expect to live mediocre while being an alpha male, which means many alpha males will start their own business and become extremely successful. When you're taking all these high-risk, high reward chances, then you will be judged by many. One of the things of becoming an alpha male is that you don't listen to anybody, and you do whatever you feel is right.

Numerous people will judge all the actions that you are going to be taking, once you're an alpha male, you will not care about other people's opinion, and you will make it happen for yourself. Which means whatever your friends and family say about your latest endeavors, you will still do whatever it is that you want to do. As you don't want to live with any regrets, living with regrets as one of the most pathetic things you can do to yourself. Which is why alphas don't do it, if you truly want to be alpha then you will not listen to anybody, and you will do whatever it is that you want to do. Another thing when it comes to becoming an alpha male is that people want to be around you. When you're an alpha male people want to be around you and understand what the hell you are doing with your life, they want to live like you, and I want to be like you.

Now, this success will be achieved later on in your life when you become extremely successful in whatever that is, you're doing. However, this is one of the biggest signs of becoming an alpha male. You will truly know that you became an alpha male when you understand that people who want to be like you hang around you. They want to learn from you and understand how it is that you live your life, which is one of the biggest compliments and the biggest signs are you going to be an alpha male.

And as always, you help them out understanding what they should be doing with their lives and how to make it happen for them. Make sure you help them out as it will be rewarding for you at the end of the day, and as always recognize who is around you for the right reasons and who is around you for the wrong reasons.

When you're an alpha male people know you, people recognize who you are and will always compliment to you with the things that you're doing. This isn't so hard to achieve, if you're really focused on the work that you were going to be doing people in the workforce will understand you and see you as an alpha male. One of the biggest things is becoming an alpha male is being focused at what you're doing, so if you're an architect make sure that you're building the best buildings possible and really being focused on what you're doing.

That way, when you enter in an architecture firm, everybody will know who you are and will treat you like a champ since you will be doing everything possible to become an alpha male. An alpha male knows how to understand his emotions, if you're an alpha male, then you will know when to act a certain way when it comes to expressing emotions. Many people disregard this point, but it is one of the most important points when it comes to becoming an alpha male. If you want to become an alpha male, then you need to make sure that you are doing everything properly in your life to become one. And you cannot neglect the part of being emotionally intelligent, which means you need to understand how to treat others based on their emotions.

Emotions are one of the strongest things to humankind, which is why you need to treat people who are extremely emotional differently, and people who are emotionally numb differently. This will give you a great balance on working with everybody else, which brings me to another point. Alpha males are really good at working with other people and to understand their needs. When you're an alpha male, you're the boss, which means you know how to read other people and work with together. So, once you have your own company and you're making a lot of money, then you will be able to gauge that off by working with other people and to know how to treat them properly.

This is where emotional intelligence comes in, you will be working in a perfect, emotionally balanced workplace, helping people accordingly to achieve their goals in your company. Being an alpha male, as we said before, is to help other people grow, so make sure you do that. Another great sign of becoming an alpha male is that you inspire others. Many people don't know this but the people you inspired by are the most likely alpha male, and you don't just do that by your work but by your actions. People will most likely forget what you tell them. However, your actions will speak for themselves. For example, if you're into working out and you want to look really buff on the beach, you can tell all your friends all about it how you're going to get there.

Once you get, there will be a completely different story when it comes to showing the results, once people see results, they will start liking you even more and will want to become your friend. More specifically will be inspired by you to become whatever it is that you want to be, which is one of the biggest signs of being an alpha male.

Speaking of getting buff, one of the most important things of becoming an alpha male is that you take care of yourself on the way you look. You need to make sure that you're looking really good and you're presentable when you're an alpha male, appearance does matter unlike many people say. When you walk into the room, we need to make sure that you leave a presence, and for you to have a great presentation, you need to make sure that you look a lot better in person and you take care of yourself. This does not mean that you have to be the best-looking guy in the world, but you need to make sure that you are well groomed and dressed properly.

Let's face it, you cannot be looking like a homeless person every day if you want to become an alpha male.

Make sure they take care of your dressing sense, and you grooming style. Unlike many people might say, people do judge a book by its cover, so make sure they cover is really nice and pretty. Finally, when it comes to becoming an alpha male, people want to be like you. Even the people who hate you would love to trade places with you. Here's the thing once you become an alpha male, there's going to be a lot of haters. The reason behind it is because everybody wants to become you, but it is impossible for them to get there because they don't have the same mental capacity as you. This is one of the great things about becoming an alpha male.

Once you become an alpha male, you will see the benefits of how people treat you and how you're going to be successful, more specifically you will start to see your haters really hate you and try to mimic you based on that. This is perhaps the best compliment you will ever get if people hate you and want to be like you then you are an alpha male. With that being said hopefully, this gives you a better idea on what an alpha male truly is and what points need to look out for when you become one. This is just a basic idea on what alpha male looks like, although with amazing points. Hopefully, this chapter really helped you foresee what the whole book is going to be about, see you in the next chapter.

Chapter 2: What is the Habits of an Alpha Male

If you can tell by the title of this book, you can say that being an alpha male has profoundly influenced this book and how we want to function. Alpha males are one of the most "well oiled" living things out there, and we can learn a lot from them in regard to becoming successful in our \own field. With that being said, how we can become more successful with the help of our habits. Well one of the main things an alpha male has going for them is consistency and the power of practices, in this chapter we are going to talk about what habits really are and how to develop good ones. This will allow you to become better functioning in your task, which is what the whole point of this book is. With that being said, this chapter may come off as long are theoretical chapter. Just be aware of the fact that we have tried to make this book as information dense as possible, and although some might find the things listed in this chapter not as exciting as the other ones, just remember that habit as are very crucial when it comes to becoming an alpha male.

Before we get into the topic of "why habits are crucial," let's talk about what is a habit. Merely put a habit is a tendency or practice that a person does on a regular base, especially when it hard for them to give up. It could be something simple, like having your morning cup of Joe or brushing your teeth, and those are the habits that you do on a regular base. Now not that I would ask you to do this, but if I were to tell you to give up brushing your teeth for twenty-one days I am hoping most of the readers would find it hard to do so as it is a habit. Since most of the actions we do on a day to day basis our practices get even stronger as we do it for a more extended period of time and on top of that they become automatic, so also if you are trying to give up your habit continuously your subconscious mind will make it harder for you as you would be programmed to do a particular task preemptively.

As you can see, the sooner you make your "good" habits automatic, the better it will be for you. You might be thinking about how someone can become so dependent on habits it is simple. When someone has developed a habit, your brain's neurological system starts craving the patterns you have created. Whenever you take part in a specific task which is now a habit, your brain releases "pleasure" chemical every-time you take part in that activity. So, by now, you can tell how habits can be so crucial. To make it easy for you to follow along, I will point out the three most important reasons as to why habits are essential.

The Reasons why habits are crucial:

- Most actions you do every day are a cause of your habit.

- The more you perform the habit, the more "second nature" it becomes.

- Good or bad, your brain releases "pleasure" chemical in your brain when you perform your habit.

After reading the points, you can see how habits can play a huge role in your day to day life. Making sure you have the right habits can make you or break you, so if you want to be more efficient with your work you need to have habits that will help you be more efficient listed in this book below. Now we have covered the topic of habits being crucial let's dive into the topic of how habits are created.

A simple trigger creates habits, we will be using a made-up scenario to explain how habits are formed. Let's say a person name John Doe is feeling depressed on a Friday night, and he is not happy with his career and other personal matters he has. But it's his friend's birthday that day, so he goes to his party when he gets there, he is offered a drink which he takes. All of a sudden, all his worries are gone, and he is living in cloud nine, this is a trigger to habits.

Then after John Doe leaves his friends party, he goes home to bed wakes up the Next day feeling even more depressed. He bears with it till the evening then decides to have a drink by himself to get rid of the feeling, as you can see it's becoming a pattern now which will be slowly turned into a routine. Soon John Doe will feel even more depressed and start drinking even more frequently the more he drinks, the better he feels, as you can see his brain is using a reward system or as we previously talked about it as your mind releasing "pleasure" chemical. Within a blink of an eye, it is now turned into a full-blown habit. Hopefully, by now you have gotten an idea of how habits are created. Let us break it down even more so its crystal clear for readers to follow.

How are habits formed:

- trigger

- Routine

- Reward

These are the three steps of how habits are created, first is the trigger which is friends party, second is the next morning when John Doe is feeling depressed and decides to have another drink which is now turned into a routine. The third one is when John Doe feels good after his drink as his "pleasure" chemical is resale and now has turned into a reward system, this is how a habit is created.

I really hope, you have gotten the idea of how important a habit can be when it comes to your daily life. Your habits really make you the person you are, and you can see our example John Doe could have made his life a lot better if he had decided to fight his depression differently had he not drank at his friend's party. Habits are created, and they tend to sneak up on you, so you as a reader need to be aware of what you are about to do and when, as it can be a trigger to a bad habit. This book is about how to make your life better with the use of habits, which will make you more efficient at your work/craft. I will be laying down the habits later in this book to be more efficient, but in order for you to be more efficient you need to get rid of habits that are going to hinder your success, now I can't tell you which habit of yours is a bad habit that you need to get away of, but what I want you to do is find out for yourself what is holding you back. Get rid of it, the sooner you do it, the better

How to get rid of bad habits

We had discussed how habits are crucial when it comes to being more efficient. Later, we dove into the topic of how bad habits can jeopardize your chances of getting into better habits. That being said, there is no winning being in a habit that is holding you back, it can be physically unhealthy for you to continue on with this habit. Not only that it can also be time-consuming, but you even should not be wasting your energy on it. We have seen this over and over again people waste their time and energy on doing stuff that they should not be doing based on their goals, and the worst part is they know that but still decide to continue on with their bad habit. Now in the previous chapter, I had advised you to find out for yourself your bad habits. When you have discovered your bad habits, I want you to go thru these steps/methods to get rid of them. In order for you to really be more efficient and get the most off of the techniques in this book, you need to get rid of the habits that are holding you back.

That being said let us discuss the first method. The first method when it comes to getting rid of your bad habit is to replace it. So, if your bad habit is drinking alcohol on a regular basis as this habit helps you escape reality, then instead of completely cutting out this habit introduce a new habit which will help replace this habit perhaps meditation. Slowly decrease the number of drinks you have by compensating them with the use of meditation or any other helpful habit you prefer.

Another method to get rid of your bad habit which I think is really important if you want to be successful is to cut out all the triggers that cause you to indulge in those habits. So again, if your bad habit is drinking alcohol, then stop going to bars and clubs with your friends as it will only make it harder for you to give up your bad habit. Most of the time people indulge in their bad habits just because they have a trigger or an excuse to do so, if your bad habit was drinking alcohol, and you decided to go out with your friends on the weekend, there is a really high chance you will let loose and have a couple of drinks so in order for you to cut out bad habit you need to get rid of all the triggers.

Now, the next one should be easy for you to do. I want you to get a family member or a close friend to check up on you even week or as often as they, let them know you want to give up a particular habit and you need someone to hold you accountable it. This method will really help you stay on top your endeavors of giving up your bad habit and help you get closer to your goal of giving up your bad habit.

The final method that will really help you stay strong during these methods it to know you will fail. There will be times where you decide to indulge in your bad habit, but that's ok start back up again you will get stronger mentally the more times you fail. The faster you realize you are going to fail the better chances you have of giving up your habit. That being said follow all these steps and you should be on the path of giving up your bad habit.

Strategies to give up bad habits:
- Replace your bad habit

- Avoid all the triggers

- Have someone hold you accountable for the things you do

- Be prepared to fail

One thing you should always remember to do is slowly give up your habit, so slowly lower the number of times you indulge in those habits and replace them with a good habit just like we talked about. I don't recommend you give up your addiction cold turkey as it has a higher chance of you giving up completely, the key to success when giving up a habit is slow constant change. If you follow the methods, I have listed in this chapter to give up your habits, you should be on your way to completely give up your bad habit. That being said once you get to a point where you are not indulging in those and habit, don't indulge in them at all until you have lost the craving. Trust me to follow these steps, and you will give up your bad habits.

To conclude this section, remember no one is perfect everyone has their bad habits. But if those bad habits are affecting our potential to have a better life, then it is about time we get rid of those habits or replace them with something better for us. Most of you guys reading this book want to be successful but in order to be successful you need to get rid of thing that are holding you back, once you have gotten rid of all the habits that are holding you back you will gain some good habits that successful people follow and do to be more successful and have a better life.

Let's face it we have bad habits to escape reality, but reality is where we live we procrastinate and dream about having a great experience when we can get rid of procrastination and have an excellent life for real the choice is yours either you start building great habits and have the life you want or keep up with your bad habits and live at the life you want in your closed imaginary world.

Early riser

Waking up early is a pretty significant step when it comes to bettering yourself, more specifically being more efficient. If you were to ask any well-off person if they wake up early or not, their answer would be YES, they are. That being said, even from personal experience, it has made me a lot more productive. If you want to better your life and live a more productive/efficient life, then you need to train yourself to become an early riser. That being said its easier said than done for most of us to wake up early, in the beginning, you will be groggy and tired, but once your body gets used to waking up early you will see benefits like:

- More time to get other important things

- Your mind will be well-rested in the mornings

- Early risers tend to be better at planning goals and making decisions

As you can see there are a lot of benefits to waking up early, this habit will definitely be a great point for you. It will make you more productive and more efficient in your life. If you have goals and visions for yourself, then you need to implement this habit right now. Waking up early can provide you with some health benefits.

Helps with better mental health

Most people don't realize how much waking up early can help with mental health. The way you get started on your day is crucial as it can affect your whole day. First, by waking up early can help you reduce the likelihood of you rushing out the door. If you wake up early, you have more time to take it easy and take your time with a tedious task which will help you stay calm and collective during the day. This will make a big difference when your calm and not rushing out the door you will be in a more enhanced mood which will help you do better work, it a win-win situation for you. Also, studies are showing that people who are early risers tend to be more positive than people who aren't, which is excellent you being positive and being in a positive mood will really help you with the quality of life you are living, which should be our goal to better our life. So not only will you not be rushing to work/school, but you will also become more positive, this benefit alone would turn me on to the idea of waking up early.

More time to workout

As we know, it is essential to stay in shape and live a healthier life if you want to live a better life. Now since you wake up earlier in the morning, you soon will have more time to get a workout in which kind of kills two birds with one stone, you wake up early and you get yourself healthy. Not only that after your workout you will have more time to prepare a healthy breakfast for yourself and start the day of the right way.

Helps with the quality of your sleep
Since you will be walking up early, you probably will be going to bed earlier also which means you will have developed a specific sleeping pattern. Once you have a sleep pattern, you will notice that your sleep gets deeper, which means you will be well rested in the morning. See, our primary goal is to set your natural clock to wake up and go to bed at the same time each day. This will help us wake up early and wake up a lot more refreshed the next morning so make sure you establish a sleeping pattern to wake up early and going to bed early every day, and it is healthy for you.

Helps you enjoy quality time
Waking up early will help you have some time to yourself, which means you can have some quality time to get the important things done in a calm and relaxed way as there is no urgency. When you have more time on your hand, you tend to be a lot calmer which will help you stay calm and have a lot less stress. In the long term, having some quality time to yourself will help you lower your stress overall which will make you a happier person, which will further help you to become more productive and efficient at your work.

Now as you can see, waking up early is a fantastic habit to have none the less. But easier said than done waking up early can be hard for most readers, as some of us will find excuses to not wake up early each and every day. At this point, you will only need to have some will power and just get up early and not press the snooze button. Just find it within you like the famous Nike phrase says "just do it" trust me it's not that hard for the readers who are thinking that it is, just start getting up early and fight the grogginess for a couple of days and you will be fine as you would have set your natural clock by that point. Here are some points to remember before you start waking up early.

- Motivate yourself to get up early

- Hold yourself accountable

- Don't snooze

- Once your eyes open get out of the bed

At this point, I want you to start waking up early. In the beginning, it will require a lot of will power but the slowly you will get used to it, eventually waking up early and going to bed early will become second nature to you just be patient with this process and don't give up. After all, you know very well now, waking up early will help you tremendously which your life as it will make it better. So, don't give upkeep waking up early until it becomes second nature and start seeing yourself living a better life.

Stay Clean
When it comes to living a better life, a more productive life, and being more successful, being clean should be a habit we need to adopt. Being clean will not only keep everything hygienic, but it will also help you become more organized. This is big being organized will help you a lot when it comes to saving time, how you might ask simple when you are organized you will know

where your stuff is so no need to waste your time looking for it as you would know where it is located. So, it is crucial that we keep our surroundings clean, our home and our workplace as this will help us be more efficient in our day to day lives. Let us get into the details of how this habit will help you.

Feel Good
This is a fantastic feeling you get when you start off staying clean, when you are honest, you feel great! You are more inclined to work harder and more efficiently. Another thing with feeling good and staying clean is that it will lower stress for you, believe it or not when we are not organized, we are continually looking for our things which can stress us out during the day. Being more organized will take this stress away from you, which will make your life a lot less stressful trust me; it makes a big difference.

Staying more organized
We have already talked about this, but let's discuss this a little deeper. See when you are clean your things are in place, which means when you are working, and you want something you would know exactly where it would be. This will help you not freak out about things and therefore make you more inclined to work when you are more prone to work you are also more likely to be good at your work which means more accomplishments which will then lead to a better life, need I say more.

Boost in productivity
When you have less distraction around you, you will be able to focus more at your work which is ahead of you. You see when you have less distraction around you,

your brain will not get overwhelmed by the disturbance when we are unorganized, and we have our stuff laying around our mind gets distracted. So, less distraction around you will equal to you being more focused.

All in all, you can now see how staying clean will help you live a better life. Now we get on with starting to implement this habit, With any new pattern you start I highly recommend you start slow, meaning that don't go cold turkey as some would say as you will most likely give up trying and go back to not implementing this or any other habit listed in this book.

It is always advised to start slow and slowly taper up to a more significant commitment with the habit. So, here is how I would begin to step by step.

Start by keeping your worktable clean by organizing your things before you leave

Slowly scale up everyday room by room until you can keep your whole house/apartment clean

Repeat this process every time things start getting out of order.
Keep following these steps, until keeping things clean become a second nature habit to you. In the beginning, it will be hard to keep things clean every time they are unorganized but keep doing it! It will become a habit which helps you to become a better person, plus who likes to live or work in a mess.

In conclusion, staying clean will help you with a lot of things like we talked about. You are keeping things fresh in your house will not only help you to be better at your work, but it will also keep you happier and less stressed. Nowadays, the world we live in being happy and having less stress is something we as human beings can benefit from. Staying clean will give you something priceless which is less stress and will to work, as you will be cleaned you will become more organized which will only make it easy for you to scale up your work in less time. Since you will be not looking for things, as you will know where what is which is the main reason why your work will scale up fast at a short period. Now let's put work aside, when you keep things clean you will most likely not get you sick so often as you will be a lot more hygienic, which will eliminate sick days, which is good! Bad if you work for a company and have to use up your sick days. If that's the case, then act ill and make it your day to have fun.

Another thing about staying clean is that people around will notice it and appreciate it. When people come to your house, the first thing they notice is how clean the house is, if your home is clean then people will appreciate that for sure. You don't want to go to someone's house who does keep it clean, am I right? It might be hard, in the beginning, to stay clean, but trust me to keep up any it, and you will make this your habit.

END OF PREVIEW